CAMBRIDGE
LEARNING CENTER
OF NEW JERSEY

ISBN# **978-1718673106**

WORD:

Superfluous

What it means:

more than needed, extra, unnecessary

What part of speech is this word?

adjective

What are 2 synonyms for this word?

extra, too much

USE THE WORD IN A SENTENCE:

I packed a superfluous amount of clothes for the trip.

IS THERE A PICTURE THAT CAN HELP YOU REMEMBER WHAT THIS WORD MEANS?

WORD:

Sufficient

What it means:

to have plenty of, enough

I
s

What part of speech is this word?

adjective

What are 2 synonyms for this word?

ample, enough

USE THE WORD IN A SENTENCE:

We had sufficient amount of food to eat for dinner.

IS THERE A PICTURE THAT CAN HELP YOU REMEMBER WHAT THIS WORD MEANS?

WORD:

hubris

What it means:

excessive pride or self-confidence

What part of speech is this word?

noun

What are 2 synonyms for this word?

pride

USE THE WORD IN A SENTENCE:

She aced all her other tests so she was filled with hubris and didn't study for the last one.

IS THERE A PICTURE THAT CAN HELP YOU REMEMBER WHAT THIS WORD MEANS?

4

WORD:

defiant

What it means:

boldly resistant or challenging

What part of speech is this word?

adjective

What are 2 synonyms for this word?

daring and rebellious

USE THE WORD IN A SENTENCE:

Taking caring of younger children can be defiant.

IS THERE A **PICTURE** THAT CAN HELP YOU REMEMBER WHAT THIS WORD MEANS?

WORD:

secession

What it means:

to withdraw formally from an alliance, federation, or association, as from a political union, a religious organization, etc.

What part of speech is this word?

Verb

What are 2 synonyms for this word?

USE THE WORD IN A SENTENCE:

IS THERE A PICTURE THAT CAN HELP YOU REMEMBER WHAT THIS WORD MEANS?

WORD:

Predecessor

What it means:

people who came before

What part of speech is this word?

noun and adjective

What are 2 synonyms for this word?

antecedent, ancestors

USE THE WORD IN A SENTENCE:

My predecessors share many stories about their predecessors.

IS THERE A PICTURE THAT CAN HELP YOU REMEMBER WHAT THIS WORD MEANS?

They were great people.

WORD:

Fortuitous

What it means:

Happening by luck or accident

What part of speech is this word?

adjective

What are 2 synonyms for this word?

Lucky / accidential

USE THE WORD IN A SENTENCE:

IS THERE A PICTURE THAT CAN HELP YOU REMEMBER WHAT THIS WORD MEANS?

WORD:

vigorous

What it means:

Strong, healthy, and full of energy

What part of speech is this word?

adjective

What are 2 synonyms for this word?

USE THE WORD IN A SENTENCE:

IS THERE A PICTURE THAT CAN HELP YOU REMEMBER WHAT THIS WORD MEANS?

WORD:

eFFusive

What it means:

expressing feeling of gratitude or happiness

What part of speech is this word?

verb

What are 2 synonyms for this word?

USE THE WORD IN A SENTENCE:

IS THERE A PICTURE THAT CAN HELP YOU REMEMBER WHAT THIS WORD MEANS?

WORD:

extolling

What it means:

to praise enthusiastically

What part of speech is this word?

verb

What are 2 synonyms for this word?

USE THE WORD IN A SENTENCE:

IS THERE A PICTURE THAT CAN HELP YOU REMEMBER WHAT THIS WORD MEANS?

WORD:

catalyst

What it means:

something that speeds up something

What part of speech is this word?

noun

What are 2 synonyms for this word?

enzyme, impulse

USE THE WORD IN A SENTENCE:

He pushed the bicycle to give it more catalyst.

IS THERE A PICTURE THAT CAN HELP YOU REMEMBER WHAT THIS WORD MEANS?

WORD:

proliferation

What it means:

spread throughout

What part of speech is this word?

noun

What are 2 synonyms for this word?

generation, expansion

USE THE WORD IN A SENTENCE:

As time goes by more proliferation occurs.

IS THERE A PICTURE THAT CAN HELP YOU REMEMBER WHAT THIS WORD MEANS?

1900

2000

WORD:

homage

What it means:

respect or reverence paid

What part of speech is this word?

noun

What are 2 synonyms for this word?

adoration, awe

USE THE WORD IN A SENTENCE:

In her speech she gave Oprah homage.

IS THERE A PICTURE THAT CAN HELP YOU REMEMBER WHAT THIS WORD MEANS?

She is a wonderful women.

WORD:
Prudence

What it means:

When you do what is reasonable.

What part of speech is this word?

noun

What are 2 synonyms for this word?

care, concern

USE THE WORD IN A SENTENCE:

She always has prudence with what she is doing.

IS THERE A **PICTURE** THAT CAN HELP YOU REMEMBER WHAT THIS WORD MEANS?

WORD:
tranquility

What it means:
Calm, peaceful

What part of speech is this word?
noun

What are 2 synonyms for this word?
Composure, coolness

USE THE WORD IN A SENTENCE:
Even in stressful situations she has tranquility.

IS THERE A PICTURE THAT CAN HELP YOU REMEMBER WHAT THIS WORD MEANS?

Exhale
Inhale

WORD:

imposition

What it means:

the laying on of something as a burden '

What part of speech is this word?

noun

What are 2 synonyms for this word?

con, fraud

USE THE WORD IN A SENTENCE:

He was an imposition of the real person who was suppose to be.

IS THERE A **PICTURE** THAT CAN HELP YOU REMEMBER WHAT THIS WORD MEANS?

WORD:

naiveté

What it means:

a naive action

What part of speech is this word?

noun

What are 2 synonyms for this word?

frankness, naturalness

USE THE WORD IN A SENTENCE:

No one believed what he did was naiveté.

IS THERE A PICTURE THAT CAN HELP YOU REMEMBER WHAT THIS WORD MEANS?

I promise I didn't!

I don't believe that!

WORD #20 (TIME FOR A QUIZ!)

advocate

What it means:

to speak or write in favor

What part of speech is this word?

verb

What are 2 synonyms for this word?

attorney, defender

His supporters advocated him.

IS THERE A PICTURE THAT CAN HELP YOU REMEMBER WHAT THIS WORD MEANS?

WORD:

hampered

What it means:

hinder or impede
the movement or
progress of

What part of speech is this word?

verb

What are 2 synonyms for this word?

baffle, check

USE THE WORD IN A SENTENCE:

The rain hampered
their playtime.

IS THERE A PICTURE THAT CAN HELP YOU REMEMBER WHAT THIS WORD MEANS?

WORD:

inquisitive

What it means:

given to inquiry, research, or asking questions

What part of speech is this word?

adjective

What are 2 synonyms for this word?

challenging, forward

USE THE WORD IN A SENTENCE:

She is, inquisitive person.
a

USE THE WORD IN A SENTENCE:

IS THERE A **PICTURE** THAT CAN HELP YOU REMEMBER WHAT THIS WORD MEANS?

What is that?

WORD:

Skepticism

What it means:

doubt

What part of speech is this word?

noun

What are 2 synonyms for this word?

disbelief, distrust

USE THE WORD IN A SENTENCE:

He had skepticism about the case.

IS THERE A **PICTURE** THAT CAN HELP YOU REMEMBER WHAT THIS WORD MEANS?

WORD:

Vigorously

What it means:

Strong, active

What part of speech is this word?

adjective

What are 2 synonyms for this word?

boldly, eagerly

USE THE WORD IN A SENTENCE:

He is vigorously running.

IS THERE A PICTURE THAT CAN HELP YOU REMEMBER WHAT THIS WORD MEANS?

WORD:

sedentary

What it means:

motionless, lazy

What part of speech is this word?

adjective

What are 2 synonyms for this word?

seated, desk

USE THE WORD IN A SENTENCE:

He was in a
sedentary occupation.

IS THERE A PICTURE THAT CAN HELP YOU REMEMBER WHAT THIS WORD MEANS?

WORD:

Slothful

What it means:

indolent, lazy

What part of speech is this word?

adjective

What are 2 synonyms for this word?

dull, inactive

USE THE WORD IN A SENTENCE:

He is very slothful.

IS THERE A PICTURE THAT CAN HELP YOU REMEMBER WHAT THIS WORD MEANS?

WORD:

resolute

What it means:

firmly resolved

What part of speech is this word?

adjective

What are 2 synonyms for this word?

bold, courageous

USE THE WORD IN A SENTENCE:

She is very courageous,

IS THERE A PICTURE THAT CAN HELP YOU REMEMBER WHAT THIS WORD MEANS?

← mountain

WORD:

explicitly

What it means:

fully and clearly expressed

What part of speech is this word?

adjective

What are 2 synonyms for this word?

absolutely, clearly

USE THE WORD IN A SENTENCE:

She explicitly stated her opinion.

IS THERE A PICTURE THAT CAN HELP YOU REMEMBER WHAT THIS WORD MEANS?

WORD:

altruistic

What it means:

doing something out of the kindess of your heart

What part of speech is this word?

adjective.

What are 2 synonyms for this word?

caring, kind act

USE THE WORD IN A SENTENCE:

She helpsout at the homeless shelter altruisticly.

IS THERE A PICTURE THAT CAN HELP YOU REMEMBER WHAT THIS WORD MEANS?

29

WORD:

permeated

What it means:

to pass into or through every part of

What part of speech is this word?

verb

What are 2 synonyms for this word?

charge, filter

USE THE WORD IN A SENTENCE:

The sunlight permeated throughout the room.

IS THERE A PICTURE THAT CAN HELP YOU REMEMBER WHAT THIS WORD MEANS?

WORD:

Utter

What it means:

to give audible expression to

What part of speech is this word?

verb

What are 2 synonyms for this word?

speak ; pronounce

USE THE WORD IN A SENTENCE:

She was unable to utter her emotions.

IS THERE A PICTURE THAT CAN HELP YOU REMEMBER WHAT THIS WORD MEANS?

WORD:
class (and meaning)

What part of speech is this word?

the system of dividing society | noun

What are 2 synonyms for this word?

caste; social rank

USE THE WORD IN A SENTENCE:

He is rich, which make him part of high class.

IS THERE A **PICTURE** THAT CAN HELP YOU REMEMBER WHAT THIS WORD MEANS?

I have cars, a boat, 2 homes, and lots of money!

WORD:

Commune

What it means:

to converse or talk together

What part of speech is this word?

Verb

What are 2 synonyms for this word?

collective, family

USE THE WORD IN A SENTENCE:

She commune with nature.

IS THERE A PICTURE THAT CAN HELP YOU REMEMBER WHAT THIS WORD MEANS?

WORD:

flux

What it means:

a flowing or flow

What part of speech is this word?

noun

What are 2 synonyms for this word?

cnange, flow

USE THE WORD IN A SENTENCE:

Her view of the show flux,

IS THERE A PICTURE THAT CAN HELP YOU REMEMBER WHAT THIS WORD MEANS?

WORD:

insurgency

What it means:

the state or condition of being insurgent

What part of speech is this word?

noun

What are 2 synonyms for this word?

revolt, mutiny

USE THE WORD IN A SENTENCE:

He was insurgency.

IS THERE A **PICTURE** THAT CAN HELP YOU REMEMBER WHAT THIS WORD MEANS?

WORD:

Staunch

What it means:

Characterized by firmness, steadfastness, or loyalty

What part of speech is this word?

adjective

What are 2 synonyms for this word?

faithful, loyal

USE THE WORD IN A SENTENCE:

He is a staunch friend.

IS THERE A PICTURE THAT CAN HELP YOU REMEMBER WHAT THIS WORD MEANS?

WORD:

reluctant

What it means:

Unwilling

What part of speech is this word?

adjective

What are 2 synonyms for this word?

afraid, cautious

USE THE WORD IN A SENTENCE:

She is very reluctant.

IS THERE A PICTURE THAT CAN HELP YOU REMEMBER WHAT THIS WORD MEANS?

WORD:

infer

What it means:

to guess; speculate

What part of speech is this word?

Verb

What are 2 synonyms for this word?

assume; collect

USE THE WORD IN A SENTENCE:

We can infer the answer is B.

IS THERE A PICTURE THAT CAN HELP YOU REMEMBER WHAT THIS WORD MEANS?

WORD:

injustice

What it means:

the quality or fact of being unjust.

What part of speech is this word?

noun

What are 2 synonyms for this word?

abuse; crime.

USE THE WORD IN A SENTENCE:

That is an act of injustice.

IS THERE A PICTURE THAT CAN HELP YOU REMEMBER WHAT THIS WORD MEANS?

No littering

WORD#40 (TIME FOR QUIZ):

tyrant

What it means:

a sovereign or other ruler who
uses power unjustly

What part of speech is this word?

noun

What are 2 synonyms for this word?

absolute ruler, bully

USE THE WORD IN A SENTENCE:

That country's new president
is a tyrant.

IS THERE A **PICTURE** THAT CAN HELP YOU REMEMBER WHAT THIS WORD MEANS?

Bow
Down
to
me

WORD:

Sniveling

What it means:

to weep or cry with Sniffling

What part of speech is this word?

verb

What are 2 synonyms for this word?

whine, cry

USE THE WORD IN A SENTENCE:

She lost her toy so she was sniveling.

IS THERE A PICTURE THAT CAN HELP YOU REMEMBER WHAT THIS WORD MEANS?

Lost & Found

WORD:

brute

What it means:

a brutal, insensitive, or crude person

What part of speech is this word?

noun

What are 2 synonyms for this word?

very strong; animal-like

USE THE WORD IN A SENTENCE:

The bodyguard was very brute.

IS THERE A PICTURE THAT CAN HELP YOU REMEMBER WHAT THIS WORD MEANS?

2

WORD:

Squabble

What it means:

to engage in a petty quarrel

What part of speech is this word?

verb

What are 2 synonyms for this word?

argument; dispute

USE THE WORD IN A SENTENCE:

They got mad at each other and started a squabble

IS THERE A PICTURE THAT CAN HELP YOU REMEMBER WHAT THIS WORD MEANS?

3

WORD:

ignoramus

What it means:

an extremely ignorant person

What part of speech is this word?

noun

What are 2 synonyms for this word?

simpleton, fool

USE THE WORD IN A SENTENCE:

He doesn't know anything he is such an ignoramus.

IS THERE A PICTURE THAT CAN HELP YOU REMEMBER WHAT THIS WORD MEANS?

4

WORD:

blasphemy

What it means:

forbidden, foolish language

What part of speech is this word?

noun

What are 2 synonyms for this word?

abuse; irreverence

USE THE WORD IN A SENTENCE:

He spoke blasphemy.

IS THERE A PICTURE THAT CAN HELP YOU REMEMBER WHAT THIS WORD MEANS?

5

WORD:

Oppressed

What it means:

to weigh down

What part of speech is this word?

verb

What are 2 synonyms for this word?

downtrodden; a slave to

USE THE WORD IN A SENTENCE:

They oppressed her from pursing her goals.

IS THERE A PICTURE THAT CAN HELP YOU REMEMBER WHAT THIS WORD MEANS?

6

WORD:

reproach

What it means:

to find fault with

What part of speech is this word?

verb

What are 2 synonyms for this word?

blame; abuse

USE THE WORD IN A SENTENCE:

He reproached me in every single thing I did.

IS THERE A PICTURE THAT CAN HELP YOU REMEMBER WHAT THIS WORD MEANS?

WORD:

Ostentatious

What it means:

designed to impress or attract notice

What part of speech is this word?

adjective

What are 2 synonyms for this word?

Showy; garnish

USE THE WORD IN A SENTENCE:

Her dress was very ostentatious.

IS THERE A PICTURE THAT CAN HELP YOU REMEMBER WHAT THIS WORD MEANS?

8

WORD#100: TIME FOR A QUIZ!

ballads

What it means:

a peom or song narrating a story in a short
stanzas

What part of speech is this word?

noun

What are 2 synonyms for this word?

song; folk song

USE THE WORD IN A SENTENCE:

They sang many ballads back in the old days.

IS THERE A **PICTURE** THAT CAN HELP YOU REMEMBER WHAT THIS WORD MEANS?

9

WRITING JOURNAL BEGINS HERE

WRITING PROMPTS BY GRADE LEVEL

I) Grade 2-4 Writing Prompts

a. Imagine you had a hundred dollars, but you couldn't keep it. You had to give it away to a person or charity. Who would you give it to? What would you want them to do with it?

b. Describe one time when you were brave.

c. Describe a time that you made a mistake and learned a lesson from your mistake. What did you learn?

d. If you could cook any meal for your family, what would you cook? Describe the meal and tell how you would make it.

e. Imagine you woke up and saw a dinosaur in your backyard. Write a story telling what you see and do.

f.   Imagine you opened your own restaurant. Tell the name of your restaurant. Explain what the restaurant looks like, who works there, and what you serve.

g.   Describe your favorite character from a book, a movie, or television.

h.   Write a story titled, "My Journey on a Pirate Ship." You and your friends can star in the story.

i.   If you could have any animal for a pet, what would it be? Describe the pet and how you would take care of it.

j.   Who is your best friend? Describe him or her.

k.   Do you have any brothers or sisters? If you do, tell what they're like. If not, tell whether or not you would like to have a brother or sister.

l.   If you could have lunch with any famous person who would it be? What would you talk about with this person?

m. Write a story titled, "The Bat Who Couldn't Fly."

n. Imagine you were a wonderful painter and your parents would let you paint anything you wanted on your bedroom walls. What would you paint? Use lots of details to describe your artwork.

o. Describe the oldest person you know.

p. Describe the youngest person you know.

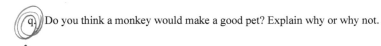

q. Do you think a monkey would make a good pet? Explain why or why not.

r. How old were you four years ago? Describe some things you can do now that you could not do then.

s. Imagine you worked at a football stadium. What would your job be? (examples: quarterback, cheerleader, coach, referee, ticket seller) Describe what you would do while you were on the job.

t. What do you like best about your home?

u. If you could be on any game show, what would it be? Describe what happens when you're on the show.

v. Describe your favorite season (fall, spring, summer, or winter). Tell what kinds of things you like to do during that season.

w. Write a story titled, "The Baby Dragon."

x. Describe several ways a person your age can earn money.

y. Would you want to visit the moon? Why or why not?

z. If you could spend an afternoon with one member of your extended family, who would it be? Tell why you chose this person and tell what you do together.

aa. Which superpower would you most like to have-- invisibility, super strength, or the ability to fly? Describe what kinds of things you would do with your powers.

bb. Think of a time when you've won something. Tell what you won and how you won it.

II) Grade 5-6 Writing Prompts

a. People often consider what it would be like to be the last person alive on earth and of course it would be horrible in lots of ways. But let us be a little different – tell me what fun you could have if the earth was all yours!?

b. Walking home from school, you see your dad stealing something from a local store. What would you do?

c. What would be your Olympic event if you had to perform at London 2012? Would you be excited or terrified!?

d. Are older people cleverer than younger people? Give reasons for your answer.

e. Can watching TV harm us?

f. Imagine being amazed and rather shocked at something you find in a drawer under your school reports. Now write about it.

g. Imagine a woman fell out of a plane flying at 20,000ft and survived. How might this have been achieved without a parachute? Use your imagination, anything goes!

h. Imagine that a lady next door digs in her garden at 3am every night. Write a about what she might be up to.

i. Is Christmas too commercialized now? What might make it better?

j. What do you feel you need to be happy?

k. If you could travel back in time, when would you go back to and why?

l. If ants ruled the world, what would things look like?

m. Imagine a lady called Denise who is a very bossy hairdresser. Eventually though she gets her comeuppance. Write about what happened.

n. If someone told you that you would be incredibly famous by the age of twenty-five, what do you think it would be for?

o. Have you ever seen something which you could just not explain?

p. Write down three facts about yourself that not many people know. Then make one fact up that could be true, but is not. Show these to your friends and see if they can spot the false fact!

q. Go and visit your eldest relation. Get them to tell you a true story their grandparents told them. This story should give you a glimpse into the past from about 100 ago. That is amazing, is it not?

r. If you could have the perfect room to do your homework in, what would it contain?

s. Find a local news story that interests you. Change one fact and re-write the story. For example, maybe a local politician opened a supermarket. What if he'd accidentally demolished it instead!

t. If it were really possible to bring dinosaurs back to life, should we?

u. Think of the oldest building you know then imagine what might be buried underneath it.

v. If a new pupil, from another town joined your school today, what one piece of advice would you give them and why?

w. Tell me about a household chore you really dislike doing.

x. Describe what it would be like to wake up from a great dream to find it was all true.

III)   <u>GRADES 7-9 WRITING PROMPTS</u>

A) Imagine you had a hundred dollars, but you couldn't keep it. You had to give it away to a person or charity. Who would you give it to? What would you want them to do with it?

B) Describe one time when you were brave.

C) If you could cook any meal for your family, what would you cook? Describe the meal and tell how you would make it.

D) Imagine you woke up and saw a dinosaur in your backyard. Write a story telling what you see and do.

E) Imagine you opened your own restaurant. Tell the name of your restaurant. Explain what the restaurant looks like, who works there, and what you serve.

F)) Describe your favorite character from a book, a movie, or television.

G) Write a story titled, "My Journey on a Pirate Ship." You and your friends can star in the story.

H) If you could have any animal for a pet, what would it be? Describe the pet and how you would take care of it.

I) Do you have any brothers or sisters? If you do, tell what they're like. If not, tell whether or not you would like to have a brother or sister.

J) If you could have lunch with any famous person who would it be? What would you talk about with this person?

K) Write a story titled, "The Bat Who Couldn't Fly."

L) Imagine you were a wonderful painter and your parents would let you paint anything you wanted on your bedroom walls. What would you paint? Use lots of details to describe your artwork.

M) Describe the oldest person you know.

N) Describe the youngest person you know.

O) Do you think a monkey would make a good pet? Explain why or why not.

P) How old were you four years ago? Describe some things you can do now that you could not do then.

Q) Imagine you worked at a football stadium. What would your job be? (examples: quarterback, cheerleader, coach, referee, ticket seller) Describe what you would do while you were on the job.

R) What do you like best about your home?

S) If you could be on any game show, what would it be? Describe what happens when you're on the show.

T) Describe your favorite season (fall, spring, summer, or winter). Tell what kinds of things you like to do during that season.

U) Write a story titled, "The Baby Dragon."

V) Describe several ways a person your age can earn money.

W) Would you want to visit the moon? Why or why not?

X) If you could spend an afternoon with one member of your extended family, who would it be? Tell why you chose this person and tell what you do together.

Y) Which superpower would you most like to have-- invisibility, super strength, or the ability to fly? Describe what kinds of things you would do with your powers.

Z) Think of a time when you've won something. Tell what you won and how you won it.

*Support opinions
*Provide evidence
*Describe
*Show, don't tell

WRITING PROMPT# 2   **Today's Date:**

TOPIC/QUESTION/ PROMPT REFERENCE #:

A monkey would be a good pet. I think this because if you love animals that are funny and love to copy you then a monkey is the pet for you. They can be a hasle to take care of but it is worth it at the end. They don't bite and can be very cute. If you are willing to take care of a human like animals then monkeys are for you. That is why a monkey could be a great pet.

Reasons why a monkey would make a bad pet

1. Hard to take care of
   - feed and *clean*
2. Noisy
3. Time consuming
* 5 paragraphs

CAMBRIDGE WRITING JOURNAL TEACHER'S RUBRIC

Rubric Standard	Grade 1-4 (4 is highest)	Specific Comments about this standard
Subject-Verb Agreement: Was there stellar *Subject-Verb* Agreement ?	/4	
Pronoun Usage: Was Pronoun Usage/Pronoun/Antecedent Agreement correct?	/4	
Vocabulary Integration: Was higher-level vocabulary used? Is the student making a good, concerted effort to use the vocabulary he/she has learned in his/her essay?	/4	
Unity & Coherence: Was the essay on topic and focused? Was there a logical progression of ideas from one to the next? Were there good transitions used in the essay to connect the different parts?	/4	
Sentence Structure and Variety: Did the essay display strong sentence structure *and* variety in sentence structure? Were there any fragments or run-on sentences?	/4	
Spelling and Correct Capitalization: How was the spelling and capitalization in the essay?	/4	
Good Opening and Closing: Were the opening and closing strong and well-stated?	/4	
Punctuation: How was the punctuation in the essay: commas, periods, semi-colons? Was it correctly implemented?	/4	
Depth of Thought and Critical Thinking: Did the student display good critical thinking, insight, and good depth of thought throughout the essay? Did he/she think "outside the box"?	/4	
Total Score	/36	

Other Feedback (Please comment on student's effort here:

_____

_____

TOPIC/QUESTION/ PROMPT REFERENCE #:

Some people may say that keeping animals in a cage is a bad thing. It can be a bad thing but, there are also many reasons why it is better to keep animals in cages. Not only will they live longer and stay healthy but, we will also get to study the animal types and species. Also, they will be a lot less frenetic than they are in the wild. Their energy will be more contained when locked in cages. That is why it would be better to keep them in cages.

The first reason why it is better to keep animals in a cage is that they will live longer and will stay healthy. If we keep a closer eye on the animals they will have a lower risk of getting sick. It is also shown in studies that animals live longer when away from the wild and under watch of humans. They would not have to worry about hunting or searching for meals. They also don't have to starve anymore if they were unsuccessful in getting food. This is because now the caretakers will feed the animals.

CAMBRIDGE WRITING JOURNAL TEACHER'S RUBRIC

Rubric Standard	Grade 1-4 (4 is highest)	Specific Comments about this standard
Subject-Verb Agreement: Was there stellar *Subject-Verb* Agreement ?	/4	
Pronoun Usage: Was Pronoun Usage/Pronoun/Antecedent Agreement correct?	/4	
Vocabulary Integration: Was higher-level vocabulary used? Is the student making a good, concerted effort to use the vocabulary he/she has learned in his/her essay?	/4	
Unity & Coherence: Was the essay on topic and focused? Was there a logical progression of ideas from one to the next? Were there good transitions used in the essay to connect the different parts?	/4	
Sentence Structure and Variety: Did the essay display strong sentence structure *and* variety in sentence structure? Were there any fragments or run-on sentences?	/4	
Spelling and Correct Capitalization: How was the spelling and capitalization in the essay?	/4	
Good Opening and Closing: Were the opening and closing strong and well-stated?	/4	
Punctuation: How was the punctuation in the essay: commas, periods, semi-colons? Was it correctly implemented?	/4	
Depth of Thought and Critical Thinking: Did the student display good critical thinking, insight, and good depth of thought throughout the essay? Did he/she think "outside the box"?	/4	
Total Score	/36	

Other Feedback (Please comment on student's effort here:

_____

_____

What do you like best about your home?

WRITING PROMPT# R   **Today's Date:** 7/17/18

TOPIC/QUESTION/ PROMPT REFERENCE #:

There are many thing that I like about about my house. For example, it's the perfect size for my family and I. However, one room in my home that is the best in my perspective is my room. It is not only decorated for my liking but, it also is a place where I can relax. Although, there may be other rooms in my home that are just as great, this is my most preferred room.

First, my room is one of the only places in my home I can relax and have peace and quiet. My little brother goes to every other room and can annoy me there*. However, my room is a place where he is not allowed to enter. Therefore he can not annoy be there. Since my room is upstairs, I don't have to worry about being bothered by all the noises downstairs. This way if my mom is cooking or my brother is watching TV. I can stay upstairs without being bothered by all the noises from downstairs.

    Next, it was decorated and painted for my liking. Every teenage girl has a

*repeating

dream room that they have alway wanted. Although,

CAMBRIDGE WRITING JOURNAL TEACHER'S RUBRIC

Rubric Standard	Grade 1-4 (4 is highest)	Specific Comments about this standard
Subject-Verb Agreement: Was there stellar *Subject-Verb* Agreement ?	/4	
Pronoun Usage: Was Pronoun Usage/Pronoun/Antecedent Agreement correct?	/4	
Vocabulary Integration: Was higher-level vocabulary used? Is the student making a good, concerted effort to use the vocabulary he/she has learned in his/her essay?	/4	
Unity & Coherence: Was the essay on topic and focused? Was there a logical progression of ideas from one to the next? Were there good transitions used in the essay to connect the different parts?	/4	
Sentence Structure and Variety: Did the essay display strong sentence structure *and* variety in sentence structure? Were there any fragments or run-on sentences?	/4	
Spelling and Correct Capitalization: How was the spelling and capitalization in the essay?	/4	
Good Opening and Closing: Were the opening and closing strong and well-stated?	/4	
Punctuation: How was the punctuation in the essay: commas, periods, semi-colons? Was it correctly implemented?	/4	
Depth of Thought and Critical Thinking: Did the student display good critical thinking, insight, and good depth of thought throughout the essay? Did he/she think "outside the box"?	/4	
Total Score	/36	

Other Feedback (Please comment on student's effort here:

_____

_____

Some immigrants to new
countries retain their language
and customs at home

TOPIC/QUESTION/ PROMPT REFERENCE #:

Some immigrants to new
countries retain their
language and customs at
home. Although, outside
of your home they may
be speaking completely
different language and
follow different customs.
It's good to follow what
you believe because
being different may
help you in life. For
example, when you go back
to your home country
you communicate with
everyone there.

Paragraph Structure

Some immigrants to new countries retain their language and customs at home. They can do this by speaking their native language with their family. Also, they can go to the temple, church, or wherever they worship to follow their customs. Lastly, they can eat and cook the food they eat from their culture and celebrate their native holidays. This way they can retain their language and customs at home in a new country.

Topic sentence

← #1 evidence

← #2

← #3

closing sentence

CAMBRIDGE WRITING JOURNAL TEACHER'S RUBRIC

Rubric Standard	Grade 1-4 (4 is highest)	Specific Comments about this standard
Subject-Verb Agreement: Was there stellar *Subject-Verb* Agreement ?	/4	
Pronoun Usage: Was Pronoun Usage/Pronoun/Antecedent Agreement correct?	/4	
Vocabulary Integration: Was higher-level vocabulary used? Is the student making a good, concerted effort to use the vocabulary he/she has learned in his/her essay?	/4	
Unity & Coherence: Was the essay on topic and focused? Was there a logical progression of ideas from one to the next? Were there good transitions used in the essay to connect the different parts?	/4	
Sentence Structure and Variety: Did the essay display strong sentence structure *and* variety in sentence structure? Were there any fragments or run-on sentences?	/4	
Spelling and Correct Capitalization: How was the spelling and capitalization in the essay?	/4	
Good Opening and Closing: Were the opening and closing strong and well-stated?	/4	
Punctuation: How was the punctuation in the essay: commas, periods, semi-colons? Was it correctly implemented?	/4	
Depth of Thought and Critical Thinking: Did the student display good critical thinking, insight, and good depth of thought throughout the essay? Did he/she think "outside the box"?	/4	
Total Score	/36	

Other Feedback (Please comment on student's effort here:

_____

_____

Describe your favorite character
from a book, a movie, or T.V.

11/21/18

TOPIC/QUESTION/ PROMPT REFERENCE #:

What are some of your

favorite characters from any
book, movie, or t.v. show? If
I had to pick a character, it
would be Meredith Grey from
the show Grey's Anatomy.
There are many reason she is
my favorite character. She
is smart, diligent, and she
does not let anything get
in her way. Also, no matter
how stressed she is, she
pushes herself to do her best.
    One of the many characteristics
Meredith has is how smart
she is. From the very beginning

of the show, she has showed her fellow interns and head doctors how smart she is. She has proved many other doctors wrong and ended up being right in the end. During all the surgeries she has scrubed in on she was done the most she can to help cure the patient. She works hard to carry her mother's legacy through out the show.

That is why my favorite character is Meredith Grey from Grey's Anatomy. She works hard. She is very diligent. Finally, she doesn't let anyone get in her way. He pushes herself

to succeed. This is why she
is my favorite T.V. show
character.

CAMBRIDGE WRITING JOURNAL TEACHER'S RUBRIC

Rubric Standard	Grade 1-4 (4 is highest)	Specific Comments about this standard
Subject-Verb Agreement: Was there stellar *Subject-Verb* Agreement ?	/4	
Pronoun Usage: Was Pronoun Usage/Pronoun/Antecedent Agreement correct?	/4	
Vocabulary Integration: Was higher-level vocabulary used? Is the student making a good, concerted effort to use the vocabulary he/she has learned in his/her essay?	/4	
Unity & Coherence: Was the essay on topic and focused? Was there a logical progression of ideas from one to the next? Were there good transitions used in the essay to connect the different parts?	/4	
Sentence Structure and Variety: Did the essay display strong sentence structure *and* variety in sentence structure? Were there any fragments or run-on sentences?	/4	
Spelling and Correct Capitalization: How was the spelling and capitalization in the essay?	/4	
Good Opening and Closing: Were the opening and closing strong and well-stated?	/4	
Punctuation: How was the punctuation in the essay: commas, periods, semi-colons? Was it correctly implemented?	/4	
Depth of Thought and Critical Thinking: Did the student display good critical thinking, insight, and good depth of thought throughout the essay? Did he/she think "outside the box"?	/4	
Total Score	/36	

Other Feedback (Please comment on student's effort here:

_____

_____

There are many people and charities that I think deserve $100. If I had to pick somewhere to give a $100 to, it would be a charity. I would pick any charity no matter the cause the charity is open for. I most likely would donate to a charity that is helping cancer patients. I would probably do this because there are many poor, innocent people in the world who have cancer. Many may not be able to pay for their treatment bills. So, I would love to help in any way I possibly can. Although, there are many places I can give this money to, this is the place I would pick.

CAMBRIDGE WRITING JOURNAL TEACHER'S RUBRIC

Rubric Standard	Grade 1-4 (4 is highest)	Specific Comments about this standard
Subject-Verb Agreement: Was there stellar *Subject-Verb* Agreement ?	/4	
Pronoun Usage: Was Pronoun Usage/Pronoun/Antecedent Agreement correct?	/4	
Vocabulary Integration: Was higher-level vocabulary used? Is the student making a good, concerted effort to use the vocabulary he/she has learned in his/her essay?	/4	
Unity & Coherence: Was the essay on topic and focused? Was there a logical progression of ideas from one to the next? Were there good transitions used in the essay to connect the different parts?	/4	
Sentence Structure and Variety: Did the essay display strong sentence structure *and* variety in sentence structure? Were there any fragments or run-on sentences?	/4	
Spelling and Correct Capitalization: How was the spelling and capitalization in the essay?	/4	
Good Opening and Closing: Were the opening and closing strong and well-stated?	/4	
Punctuation: How was the punctuation in the essay: commas, periods, semi-colors? Was it correctly implemented?	/4	
Depth of Thought and Critical Thinking: Did the student display good critical thinking, insight, and good depth of thought throughout the essay? Did he/she think "outside the box"?	/4	
Total Score	/36	

Other Feedback (Please comment on student's effort here:

_____

_____

WRITING PROMPT# B   **Today's Date:**
9/24/19

TOPIC/QUESTION/ PROMPT REFERENCE #:

Being brave isn't always easy. There have been many times where I have at least tried to be brave. It's hard to be brave because you have to stay confident and believe in yourself to be brave. There are times where you have to be brave for others. Like, having to stand up to a bully for a friend or be there when they are going through a rough time.

There are also times you

Like, standing up to someone who is causing trouble. The one time I was brave was when I wanted to be altruistic and help out a friend. I had hubris and was ready to tell whoever was bothering my friend to stop. I went up to the bully and told him to stop bothering my friend and later he did.

CAMBRIDGE WRITING JOURNAL TEACHER'S RUBRIC

Rubric Standard	Grade 1-4 (4 is highest)	Specific Comments about this standard
Subject-Verb Agreement: Was there stellar *Subject-Verb* Agreement ?	/4	
Pronoun Usage: Was Pronoun Usage/Pronoun/Antecedent Agreement correct?	/4	
Vocabulary Integration: Was higher-level vocabulary used? Is the student making a good, concerted effort to use the vocabulary he/she has learned in his/her essay?	/4	
Unity & Coherence: Was the essay on topic and focused? Was there a logical progression of ideas from one to the next? Were there good transitions used in the essay to connect the different parts?	/4	
Sentence Structure and Variety: Did the essay display strong sentence structure *and* variety in sentence structure? Were there any fragments or run-on sentences?	/4	
Spelling and Correct Capitalization: How was the spelling and capitalization in the essay?	/4	
Good Opening and Closing: Were the opening and closing strong and well-stated?	/4	
Punctuation: How was the punctuation in the essay: commas, periods, semi-colors? Was it correctly implemented?	/4	
Depth of Thought and Critical Thinking: Did the student display good critical thinking, insight, and good depth of thought throughout the essay? Did he/she think "outside the box"?	/4	
Total Score	/36	

Other Feedback (Please comment on student's effort here:

WRITING PROMPT# _____ **Today's Date:** _____

TOPIC/QUESTION/ PROMPT REFERENCE #:

_____

_____

_____

_____

_____

_____

_____

_____

_____

_____

_____

_____

_____

_____

_____

_____

_____

_____

_____

CAMBRIDGE WRITING JOURNAL TEACHER'S RUBRIC

Rubric Standard	Grade 1-4 (4 is highest)	Specific Comments about this standard
Subject-Verb Agreement: Was there stellar *Subject-Verb* Agreement ?	/4	
Pronoun Usage: Was Pronoun Usage/Pronoun/Antecedent Agreement correct?	/4	
Vocabulary Integration: Was higher-level vocabulary used? Is the student making a good, concerted effort to use the vocabulary he/she has learned in his/her essay?	/4	
Unity & Coherence: Was the essay on topic and focused? Was there a logical progression of ideas from one to the next? Were there good transitions used in the essay to connect the different parts?	/4	
Sentence Structure and Variety: Did the essay display strong sentence structure *and* variety in sentence structure? Were there any fragments or run-on sentences?	/4	
Spelling and Correct Capitalization: How was the spelling and capitalization in the essay?	/4	
Good Opening and Closing: Were the opening and closing strong and well-stated?	/4	
Punctuation: How was the punctuation in the essay: commas, periods, semi-colors? Was it correctly implemented?	/4	
Depth of Thought and Critical Thinking: Did the student display good critical thinking, insight, and good depth of thought throughout the essay? Did he/she think "outside the box"?	/4	
Total Score	/36	

Other Feedback (Please comment on student's effort here:

_____

_____

_____

WRITING PROMPT# _____ **Today's Date:**

_____

TOPIC/QUESTION/ PROMPT REFERENCE #:

_____

_____

_____

_____

_____

_____

_____

_____

_____

_____

_____

_____

_____

_____

_____

_____

_____

CAMBRIDGE WRITING JOURNAL TEACHER'S RUBRIC

Rubric Standard	Grade 1-4 (4 is highest)	Specific Comments about this standard
Subject-Verb Agreement: Was there stellar *Subject-Verb* Agreement ?	/4	
Pronoun Usage: Was Pronoun Usage/Pronoun/Antecedent Agreement correct?	/4	
Vocabulary Integration: Was higher-level vocabulary used? Is the student making a good, concerted effort to use the vocabulary he/she has learned in his/her essay?	/4	
Unity & Coherence: Was the essay on topic and focused? Was there a logical progression of ideas from one to the next? Were there good transitions used in the essay to connect the different parts?	/4	
Sentence Structure and Variety: Did the essay display strong sentence structure *and* variety in sentence structure? Were there any fragments or run-on sentences?	/4	
Spelling and Correct Capitalization: How was the spelling and capitalization in the essay?	/4	
Good Opening and Closing: Were the opening and closing strong and well-stated?	/4	
Punctuation: How was the punctuation in the essay: commas, periods, semi-colons? Was it correctly implemented?	/4	
Depth of Thought and Critical Thinking: Did the student display good critical thinking, insight, and good depth of thought throughout the essay? Did he/she think "outside the box"?	/4	
Total Score	/36	

Other Feedback (Please comment on student's effort here:

_____

_____

_____

_____ .

WRITING PROMPT# _____ **Today's Date:**

_____

TOPIC/QUESTION/ PROMPT REFERENCE #:

_____

_____

_____

_____

_____

_____

_____

_____

_____

_____

_____

_____

_____

_____

_____

_____

_____

_____

CAMBRIDGE WRITING JOURNAL TEACHER'S RUBRIC

Rubric Standard	Grade 1-4 (4 is highest)	Specific Comments about this standard
Subject-Verb Agreement: Was there stellar *Subject-Verb* Agreement ?	/4	
Pronoun Usage: Was Pronoun Usage/Pronoun/Antecedent Agreement correct?	/4	
Vocabulary Integration: Was higher-level vocabulary used? Is the student making a good, concerted effort to use the vocabulary he/she has learned in his/her essay?	/4	
Unity & Coherence: Was the essay on topic and focused? Was there a logical progression of ideas from one to the next? Were there good transitions used in the essay to connect the different parts?	/4	
Sentence Structure and Variety: Did the essay display strong sentence structure *and* variety in sentence structure? Were there any fragments or run-on sentences?	/4	
Spelling and Correct Capitalization: How was the spelling and capitalization in the essay?	/4	
Good Opening and Closing: Were the opening and closing strong and well-stated?	/4	
Punctuation: How was the punctuation in the essay: commas, periods, semi-colors? Was it correctly implemented?	/4	
Depth of Thought and Critical Thinking: Did the student display good critical thinking, insight, and good depth of thought throughout the essay? Did he/she think "outside the box"?	/4	
Total Score	/36	

Other Feedback (Please comment on student's effort here:

_____

_____

_____

WRITING PROMPT# _____ **Today's Date:**

_____

TOPIC/QUESTION/ PROMPT REFERENCE #:

_____

_____

_____

_____

_____

_____

_____

_____

_____

_____

_____

_____

_____

_____

_____

_____

_____

CAMBRIDGE WRITING JOURNAL TEACHER'S RUBRIC

Rubric Standard	Grade 1-4 (4 is highest)	Specific Comments about this standard
Subject-Verb Agreement: Was there stellar *Subject-Verb* Agreement ?	/4	
Pronoun Usage: Was Pronoun Usage/Pronoun/Antecedent Agreement correct?	/4	
Vocabulary Integration: Was higher-level vocabulary used? Is the student making a good, concerted effort to use the vocabulary he/she has learned in his/her essay?	/4	
Unity & Coherence: Was the essay on topic and focused? Was there a logical progression of ideas from one to the next? Were there good transitions used in the essay to connect the different parts?	/4	
Sentence Structure and Variety: Did the essay display strong sentence structure *and* variety in sentence structure? Were there any fragments or run-on sentences?	/4	
Spelling and Correct Capitalization: How was the spelling and capitalization in the essay?	/4	
Good Opening and Closing: Were the opening and closing strong and well-stated?	/4	
Punctuation: How was the punctuation in the essay: commas, periods, semi-colors? Was it correctly implemented?	/4	
Depth of Thought and Critical Thinking: Did the student display good critical thinking, insight, and good depth of thought throughout the essay? Did he/she think "outside the box"?	/4	
Total Score	/36	

Other Feedback (Please comment on student's effort here:

_____

_____

WRITING PROMPT# _____ **Today's Date:** _____

TOPIC/QUESTION/ PROMPT REFERENCE #:

_____

_____

_____

_____

_____

_____

_____

_____

_____

_____

_____

_____

_____

_____

_____

_____

_____

_____

_____

_____

_____

_____

_____

_____

_____

_____

_____

_____

_____

_____

_____

_____

_____

_____

_____

CAMBRIDGE WRITING JOURNAL TEACHER'S RUBRIC

Rubric Standard	Grade 1-4 (4 is highest)	Specific Comments about this standard
Subject-Verb Agreement: Was there stellar *Subject-Verb* Agreement ?	/4	
Pronoun Usage: Was Pronoun Usage/Pronoun/Antecedent Agreement correct?	/4	
Vocabulary Integration: Was higher-level vocabulary used? Is the student making a good, concerted effort to use the vocabulary he/she has learned in his/her essay?	/4	
Unity & Coherence: Was the essay on topic and focused? Was there a logical progression of ideas from one to the next? Were there good transitions used in the essay to connect the different parts?	/4	
Sentence Structure and Variety: Did the essay display strong sentence structure *and* variety in sentence structure? Were there any fragments or run-on sentences?	/4	
Spelling and Correct Capitalization: How was the spelling and capitalization in the essay?	/4	
Good Opening and Closing: Were the opening and closing strong and well-stated?	/4	
Punctuation: How was the punctuation in the essay: commas, periods, semi-colors? Was it correctly implemented?	/4	
Depth of Thought and Critical Thinking: Did the student display good critical thinking, insight, and good depth of thought throughout the essay? Did he/she think "outside the box"?	/4	
Total Score	/36	

Other Feedback (Please comment on student's effort here:

_____

_____

_____
_____ .

WRITING PROMPT# _____   **Today's Date:**

_____

TOPIC/QUESTION/ PROMPT REFERENCE #:

_____

_____

_____

_____

_____

_____

_____

_____

_____

_____

_____

_____

_____

_____

CAMBRIDGE WRITING JOURNAL TEACHER'S RUBRIC

Rubric Standard	Grade 1-4 (4 is highest)	Specific Comments about this standard
Subject-Verb Agreement: Was there stellar *Subject-Verb* Agreement ?	/4	
Pronoun Usage: Was Pronoun Usage/Pronoun/Antecedent Agreement correct?	/4	
Vocabulary Integration: Was higher-level vocabulary used? Is the student making a good, concerted effort to use the vocabulary he/she has learned in his/her essay?	/4	
Unity & Coherence: Was the essay on topic and focused? Was there a logical progression of ideas from one to the next? Were there good transitions used in the essay to connect the different parts?	/4	
Sentence Structure and Variety: Did the essay display strong sentence structure *and* variety in sentence structure? Were there any fragments or run-on sentences?	/4	
Spelling and Correct Capitalization: How was the spelling and capitalization in the essay?	/4	
Good Opening and Closing: Were the opening and closing strong and well-stated?	/4	
Punctuation: How was the punctuation in the essay: commas, periods, semi-colors? Was it correctly implemented?	/4	
Depth of Thought and Critical Thinking: Did the student display good critical thinking, insight, and good depth of thought throughout the essay? Did he/she think "outside the box"?	/4	
Total Score	/36	

Other Feedback (Please comment on student's effort here:

_____

_____

_____

_____ .

WRITING PROMPT# _____   **Today's Date:**

_____

TOPIC/QUESTION/ PROMPT REFERENCE #:

_____

_____

_____

_____

_____

_____

_____

_____

_____

_____

_____

_____

_____

_____

_____

_____

CAMBRIDGE WRITING JOURNAL TEACHER'S RUBRIC

Rubric Standard	Grade 1-4 (4 is highest)	Specific Comments about this standard
Subject-Verb Agreement: Was there stellar *Subject-Verb* Agreement ?	/4	
Pronoun Usage: Was Pronoun Usage/Pronoun/Antecedent Agreement correct?	/4	
Vocabulary Integration: Was higher-level vocabulary used? Is the student making a good, concerted effort to use the vocabulary he/she has learned in his/her essay?	/4	
Unity & Coherence: Was the essay on topic and focused? Was there a logical progression of ideas from one to the next? Were there good transitions used in the essay to connect the different parts?	/4	
Sentence Structure and Variety: Did the essay display strong sentence structure *and* variety in sentence structure? Were there any fragments or run-on sentences?	/4	
Spelling and Correct Capitalization: How was the spelling and capitalization in the essay?	/4	
Good Opening and Closing: Were the opening and closing strong and well-stated?	/4	
Punctuation: How was the punctuation in the essay: commas, periods, semi-colors? Was it correctly implemented?	/4	
Depth of Thought and Critical Thinking: Did the student display good critical thinking, insight, and good depth of thought throughout the essay? Did he/she think "outside the box"?	/4	
Total Score	/36	

Other Feedback (Please comment on student's effort here:

_____

_____

WRITING PROMPT#   **Today's Date:**

TOPIC/QUESTION/ PROMPT REFERENCE #:

CAMBRIDGE WRITING JOURNAL TEACHER'S RUBRIC

Rubric Standard	Grade 1-4 (4 is highest)	Specific Comments about this standard
Subject-Verb Agreement: Was there stellar *Subject-Verb* Agreement ?	/4	
Pronoun Usage: Was Pronoun Usage/Pronoun/Antecedent Agreement correct?	/4	
Vocabulary Integration: Was higher-level vocabulary used? Is the student making a good, concerted effort to use the vocabulary he/she has learned in his/her essay?	/4	
Unity & Coherence: Was the essay on topic and focused? Was there a logical progression of ideas from one to the next? Were there good transitions used in the essay to connect the different parts?	/4	
Sentence Structure and Variety: Did the essay display strong sentence structure *and* variety in sentence structure? Were there any fragments or run-on sentences?	/4	
Spelling and Correct Capitalization: How was the spelling and capitalization in the essay?	/4	
Good Opening and Closing: Were the opening and closing strong and well-stated?	/4	
Punctuation: How was the punctuation in the essay: commas, periods, semi-colors? Was it correctly implemented?	/4	
Depth of Thought and Critical Thinking: Did the student display good critical thinking, insight, and good depth of thought throughout the essay? Did he/she think "outside the box"?	/4	
Total Score	/36	

Other Feedback (Please comment on student's effort here:

_____

_____

_____
_____ .

WRITING PROMPT# _____ **Today's Date:**
_____

TOPIC/QUESTION/ PROMPT REFERENCE #:

_____

_____

_____

_____

_____

_____

_____

_____

_____

_____

_____

_____

_____

_____

_____

_____

CAMBRIDGE WRITING JOURNAL TEACHER'S RUBRIC

Rubric Standard	Grade 1-4 (4 is highest)	Specific Comments about this standard
Subject-Verb Agreement: Was there stellar *Subject-Verb* Agreement ?	/4	
Pronoun Usage: Was Pronoun Usage/Pronoun/Antecedent Agreement correct?	/4	
Vocabulary Integration: Was higher-level vocabulary used? Is the student making a good, concerted effort to use the vocabulary he/she has learned in his/her essay?	/4	
Unity & Coherence: Was the essay on topic and focused? Was there a logical progression of ideas from one to the next? Were there good transitions used in the essay to connect the different parts?	/4	
Sentence Structure and Variety: Did the essay display strong sentence structure *and* variety in sentence structure? Were there any fragments or run-on sentences?	/4	
Spelling and Correct Capitalization: How was the spelling and capitalization in the essay?	/4	
Good Opening and Closing: Were the opening and closing strong and well-stated?	/4	
Punctuation: How was the punctuation in the essay: commas, periods, semi-colors? Was it correctly implemented?	/4	
Depth of Thought and Critical Thinking: Did the student display good critical thinking, insight, and good depth of thought throughout the essay? Did he/she think "outside the box"?	/4	
Total Score	/36	

Other Feedback (Please comment on student's effort here:

_____

_____

WRITING PROMPT# _____ **Today's Date:** _____

TOPIC/QUESTION/ PROMPT REFERENCE #:

_____

_____

_____

_____

_____

_____

_____

_____

_____

_____

_____

_____

_____

_____

_____

_____

_____

_____

CAMBRIDGE WRITING JOURNAL TEACHER'S RUBRIC

Rubric Standard	Grade 1-4 (4 is highest)	Specific Comments about this standard
Subject-Verb Agreement: Was there stellar *Subject-Verb* Agreement ?	/4	
Pronoun Usage: Was Pronoun Usage/Pronoun/Antecedent Agreement correct?	/4	
Vocabulary Integration: Was higher-level vocabulary used? Is the student making a good, concerted effort to use the vocabulary he/she has learned in his/her essay?	/4	
Unity & Coherence: Was the essay on topic and focused? Was there a logical progression of ideas from one to the next? Were there good transitions used in the essay to connect the different parts?	/4	
Sentence Structure and Variety: Did the essay display strong sentence structure *and* variety in sentence structure? Were there any fragments or run-on sentences?	/4	
Spelling and Correct Capitalization: How was the spelling and capitalization in the essay?	/4	
Good Opening and Closing: Were the opening and closing strong and well-stated?	/4	
Punctuation: How was the punctuation in the essay: commas, periods, semi-colors? Was it correctly implemented?	/4	
Depth of Thought and Critical Thinking: Did the student display good critical thinking, insight, and good depth of thought throughout the essay? Did he/she think "outside the box"?	/4	
Total Score	/36	

Other Feedback (Please comment on student's effort here:

_____

_____

WRITING PROMPT#   **Today's Date:**

TOPIC/QUESTION/ PROMPT REFERENCE #:

CAMBRIDGE WRITING JOURNAL TEACHER'S RUBRIC

Rubric Standard	Grade 1-4 (4 is highest)	Specific Comments about this standard
Subject-Verb Agreement: Was there stellar *Subject-Verb* Agreement ?	/4	
Pronoun Usage: Was Pronoun Usage/Pronoun/Antecedent Agreement correct?	/4	
Vocabulary Integration: Was higher-level vocabulary used? Is the student making a good, concerted effort to use the vocabulary he/she has learned in his/her essay?	/4	
Unity & Coherence: Was the essay on topic and focused? Was there a logical progression of ideas from one to the next? Were there good transitions used in the essay to connect the different parts?	/4	
Sentence Structure and Variety: Did the essay display strong sentence structure *and* variety in sentence structure? Were there any fragments or run-on sentences?	/4	
Spelling and Correct Capitalization: How was the spelling and capitalization in the essay?	/4	
Good Opening and Closing: Were the opening and closing strong and well-stated?	/4	
Punctuation: How was the punctuation in the essay: commas, periods, semi-colors? Was it correctly implemented?	/4	
Depth of Thought and Critical Thinking: Did the student display good critical thinking, insight, and good depth of thought throughout the essay? Did he/she think "outside the box"?	/4	
Total Score	/36	

Other Feedback (Please comment on student's effort here)

_____

_____

WRITING PROMPT# _____ **Today's Date:** _____

TOPIC/QUESTION/ PROMPT REFERENCE #:

_____

_____

_____

_____

_____

_____

_____

_____

_____

_____

_____

_____

_____

_____

_____

_____

CAMBRIDGE WRITING JOURNAL TEACHER'S RUBRIC

Rubric Standard	Grade 1-4 (4 is highest)	Specific Comments about this standard
Subject-Verb Agreement: Was there stellar *Subject-Verb* Agreement ?	/4	
Pronoun Usage: Was Pronoun Usage/Pronoun/Antecedent Agreement correct?	/4	
Vocabulary Integration: Was higher-level vocabulary used? Is the student making a good, concerted effort to use the vocabulary he/she has learned in his/her essay?	/4	
Unity & Coherence: Was the essay on topic and focused? Was there a logical progression of ideas from one to the next? Were there good transitions used in the essay to connect the different parts?	/4	
Sentence Structure and Variety: Did the essay display strong sentence structure *and* variety in sentence structure? Were there any fragments or run-on sentences?	/4	
Spelling and Correct Capitalization: How was the spelling and capitalization in the essay?	/4	
Good Opening and Closing: Were the opening and closing strong and well-stated?	/4	
Punctuation: How was the punctuation in the essay: commas, periods, semi-colors? Was it correctly implemented?	/4	
Depth of Thought and Critical Thinking: Did the student display good critical thinking, insight, and good depth of thought throughout the essay? Did he/she think "outside the box"?	/4	
Total Score	/36	

Other Feedback (Please comment on student's effort here:

_____

_____

_____

WRITING PROMPT# _____ **Today's Date:** _____

TOPIC/QUESTION/ PROMPT REFERENCE #:

_____

CAMBRIDGE WRITING JOURNAL TEACHER'S RUBRIC

Rubric Standard	Grade 1-4 (4 is highest)	Specific Comments about this standard
Subject-Verb Agreement: Was there stellar *Subject-Verb* Agreement ?	/4	
Pronoun Usage: Was Pronoun Usage/Pronoun/Antecedent Agreement correct?	/4	
Vocabulary Integration: Was higher-level vocabulary used? Is the student making a good, concerted effort to use the vocabulary he/she has learned in his/her essay?	/4	
Unity & Coherence: Was the essay on topic and focused? Was there a logical progression of ideas from one to the next? Were there good transitions used in the essay to connect the different parts?	/4	
Sentence Structure and Variety: Did the essay display strong sentence structure *and* variety in sentence structure? Were there any fragments or run-on sentences?	/4	
Spelling and Correct Capitalization: How was the spelling and capitalization in the essay?	/4	
Good Opening and Closing: Were the opening and closing strong and well-stated?	/4	
Punctuation: How was the punctuation in the essay: commas, periods, semi-colors? Was it correctly implemented?	/4	
Depth of Thought and Critical Thinking: Did the student display good critical thinking, insight, and good depth of thought throughout the essay? Did he/she think "outside the box"?	/4	
Total Score	/36	

Other Feedback (Please comment on student's effort here:

_____

_____

WRITING PROMPT#   **Today's Date:**

TOPIC/QUESTION/ PROMPT REFERENCE #:

CAMBRIDGE WRITING JOURNAL TEACHER'S RUBRIC

Rubric Standard	Grade 1-4 (4 is highest)	Specific Comments about this standard
Subject-Verb Agreement: Was there stellar *Subject-Verb* Agreement ?	/4	
Pronoun Usage: Was Pronoun Usage/Pronoun/Antecedent Agreement correct?	/4	
Vocabulary Integration: Was higher-level vocabulary used? Is the student making a good, concerted effort to use the vocabulary he/she has learned in his/her essay?	/4	
Unity & Coherence: Was the essay on topic and focused? Was there a logical progression of ideas from one to the next? Were there good transitions used in the essay to connect the different parts?	/4	
Sentence Structure and Variety: Did the essay display strong sentence structure *and* variety in sentence structure? Were there any fragments or run-on sentences?	/4	
Spelling and Correct Capitalization: How was the spelling and capitalization in the essay?	/4	
Good Opening and Closing: Were the opening and closing strong and well-stated?	/4	
Punctuation: How as the punctuation in the essay: commas, periods, semi-colors? Was it correctly implemented?	/4	
Depth of Thought and Critical Thinking: Did the student display good critical thinking, insight, and good depth of thought throughout the essay? Did he/she think "outside the box"?	/4	
Total Score	/36	

Other Feedback (Please comment on student's effort here:

_____
_____
_____
_____ .

WRITING PROMPT#   **Today's Date:**

TOPIC/QUESTION/ PROMPT REFERENCE #:

CAMBRIDGE WRITING JOURNAL TEACHER'S RUBRIC

Rubric Standard	Grade 1-4 (4 is highest)	Specific Comments about this standard
Subject-Verb Agreement: Was there stellar *Subject-Verb* Agreement ?	/4	
Pronoun Usage: Was Pronoun Usage/Pronoun/Antecedent Agreement correct?	/4	
Vocabulary Integration: Was higher-level vocabulary used? Is the student making a good, concerted effort to use the vocabulary he/she has learned in his/her essay?	/4	
Unity & Coherence: Was the essay on topic and focused? Was there a logical progression of ideas from one to the next? Were there good transitions used in the essay to connect the different parts?	/4	
Sentence Structure and Variety: Did the essay display strong sentence structure *and* variety in sentence structure? Were there any fragments or run-on sentences?	/4	
Spelling and Correct Capitalization: How was the spelling and capitalization in the essay?	/4	
Good Opening and Closing: Were the opening and closing strong and well-stated?	/4	
Punctuation: How as the punctuation in the essay: commas, periods, semi-colors? Was it correctly implemented?	/4	
Depth of Thought and Critical Thinking: Did the student display good critical thinking, insight, and good depth of thought throughout the essay? Did he/she think "outside the box"?	/4	
Total Score	/36	

Other Feedback (Please comment on student's effort here)

_____

_____

_____

_____ .

WRITING PROMPT#

Today's Date:

TOPIC/QUESTION/ PROMPT REFERENCE #:

CAMBRIDGE WRITING JOURNAL TEACHER'S RUBRIC

Rubric Standard	Grade 1-4 (4 is highest)	Specific Comments about this standard
Subject-Verb Agreement: Was there stellar *Subject-Verb* Agreement ?	/4	
Pronoun Usage: Was Pronoun Usage/Pronoun/Antecedent Agreement correct?	/4	
Vocabulary Integration: Was higher-level vocabulary used? Is the student making a good, concerted effort to use the vocabulary he/she has learned in his/her essay?	/4	
Unity & Coherence: Was the essay on topic and focused? Was there a logical progression of ideas from one to the next? Were there good transitions used in the essay to connect the different parts?	/4	
Sentence Structure and Variety: Did the essay display strong sentence structure *and* variety in sentence structure? Were there any fragments or run-on sentences?	/4	
Spelling and Correct Capitalization: How was the spelling and capitalization in the essay?	/4	
Good Opening and Closing: Were the opening and closing strong and well-stated?	/4	
Punctuation: How as the punctuation in the essay: commas, periods, semi-colors? Was it correctly implemented?	/4	
Depth of Thought and Critical Thinking: Did the student display good critical thinking, insight, and good depth of thought throughout the essay? Did he/she think "outside the box"?	/4	
Total Score	/36	

Other Feedback (Please comment on student's effort here)

_____

_____

_____

_____ .

WRITING PROMPT# _____   **Today's Date:**
                                        _____

TOPIC/QUESTION/ PROMPT REFERENCE #:

_____

_____

_____

_____

_____

_____

_____

_____

_____

_____

_____

_____

_____

_____

_____

_____

_____

CAMBRIDGE WRITING JOURNAL TEACHER'S RUBRIC

Rubric Standard	Grade 1-4 (4 is highest)	Specific Comments about this standard
Subject-Verb Agreement: Was there stellar *Subject-Verb* Agreement ?	/4	
Pronoun Usage: Was Pronoun Usage/Pronoun/Antecedent Agreement correct?	/4	
Vocabulary Integration: Was higher-level vocabulary used? Is the student making a good, concerted effort to use the vocabulary he/she has learned in his/her essay?	/4	
Unity & Coherence: Was the essay on topic and focused? Was there a logical progression of ideas from one to the next? Were there good transitions used in the essay to connect the different parts?	/4	
Sentence Structure and Variety: Did the essay display strong sentence structure *and* variety in sentence structure? Were there any fragments or run-on sentences?	/4	
Spelling and Correct Capitalization: How was the spelling and capitalization in the essay?	/4	
Good Opening and Closing: Were the opening and closing strong and well-stated?	/4	
Punctuation: How as the punctuation in the essay: commas, periods, semi-colors? Was it correctly implemented?	/4	
Depth of Thought and Critical Thinking: Did the student display good critical thinking, insight, and good depth of thought throughout the essay? Did he/she think "outside the box"?	/4	
Total Score	/36	

Other Feedback (Please comment on student's effort here)

_____

_____

_____

_____

WRITING PROMPT# _____ **Today's Date:**

_____

TOPIC/QUESTION/ PROMPT REFERENCE #:

_____

_____

_____

_____

_____

_____

_____

_____

_____

_____

_____

_____

_____

_____

_____

_____

_____

CAMBRIDGE WRITING JOURNAL TEACHER'S RUBRIC

Rubric Standard	Grade 1-4 (4 is highest)	Specific Comments about this standard
Subject-Verb Agreement: Was there stellar *Subject-Verb* Agreement ?	/4	
Pronoun Usage: Was Pronoun Usage/Pronoun/Antecedent Agreement correct?	/4	
Vocabulary Integration: Was higher-level vocabulary used? Is the student making a good, concerted effort to use the vocabulary he/she has learned in his/her essay?	/4	
Unity & Coherence: Was the essay on topic and focused? Was there a logical progression of ideas from one to the next? Were there good transitions used in the essay to connect the different parts?	/4	
Sentence Structure and Variety: Did the essay display strong sentence structure *and* variety in sentence structure? Were there any fragments or run-on sentences?	/4	
Spelling and Correct Capitalization: How was the spelling and capitalization in the essay?	/4	
Good Opening and Closing: Were the opening and closing strong and well-stated?	/4	
Punctuation: How as the punctuation in the essay: commas, periods, semi-colors? Was it correctly implemented?	/4	
Depth of Thought and Critical Thinking: Did the student display good critical thinking, insight, and good depth of thought throughout the essay? Did he/she think "outside the box"?	/4	
Total Score	/36	

Other Feedback (Please comment on student's effort here)

_____

_____

_____

_____.

WRITING PROMPT#   **Today's Date:**

TOPIC/QUESTION/ PROMPT REFERENCE #:

CAMBRIDGE WRITING JOURNAL TEACHER'S RUBRIC

Rubric Standard	Grade 1-4 (4 is highest)	Specific Comments about this standard
Subject-Verb Agreement: Was there stellar *Subject-Verb* Agreement ?	/4	
Pronoun Usage: Was Pronoun Usage/Pronoun/Antecedent Agreement correct?	/4	
Vocabulary Integration: Was higher-level vocabulary used? Is the student making a good, concerted effort to use the vocabulary he/she has learned in his/her essay?	/4	
Unity & Coherence: Was the essay on topic and focused? Was there a logical progression of ideas from one to the next? Were there good transitions used in the essay to connect the different parts?	/4	
Sentence Structure and Variety: Did the essay display strong sentence structure *and* variety in sentence structure? Were there any fragments or run-on sentences?	/4	
Spelling and Correct Capitalization: How was the spelling and capitalization in the essay?	/4	
Good Opening and Closing: Were the opening and closing strong and well-stated?	/4	
Punctuation: How as the punctuation in the essay: commas, periods, semi-colors? Was it correctly implemented?	/4	
Depth of Thought and Critical Thinking: Did the student display good critical thinking, insight, and good depth of thought throughout the essay? Did he/she think "outside the box"?	/4	
Total Score	/36	

Other Feedback (Please comment on student's effort here)

_____

_____

_____

_____ .

WRITING PROMPT# _____ **Today's Date:**

_____

TOPIC/QUESTION/ PROMPT REFERENCE #:

_____

_____
_____
_____
_____
_____
_____
_____
_____
_____
_____
_____
_____
_____
_____
_____
_____
_____
_____

CAMBRIDGE WRITING JOURNAL TEACHER'S RUBRIC

Rubric Standard	Grade 1-4 (4 is highest)	Specific Comments about this standard
Subject-Verb Agreement: Was there stellar *Subject-Verb* Agreement ?	/4	
Pronoun Usage: Was Pronoun Usage/Pronoun/Antecedent Agreement correct?	/4	
Vocabulary Integration: Was higher-level vocabulary used? Is the student making a good, concerted effort to use the vocabulary he/she has learned in his/her essay?	/4	
Unity & Coherence: Was the essay on topic and focused? Was there a logical progression of ideas from one to the next? Were there good transitions used in the essay to connect the different parts?	/4	
Sentence Structure and Variety: Did the essay display strong sentence structure *and* variety in sentence structure? Were there any fragments or run-on sentences?	/4	
Spelling and Correct Capitalization: How was the spelling and capitalization in the essay?	/4	
Good Opening and Closing: Were the opening and closing strong and well-stated?	/4	
Punctuation: How as the punctuation in the essay: commas, periods, semi-colors? Was it correctly implemented?	/4	
Depth of Thought and Critical Thinking: Did the student display good critical thinking, insight, and good depth of thought throughout the essay? Did he/she think "outside the box"?	/4	
Total Score	/36	

Other Feedback (Please comment on student's effort here)

_____

_____

_____

_____ .

WRITING PROMPT# _____ **Today's Date:**

_____

TOPIC/QUESTION/ PROMPT REFERENCE #:

_____

_____

_____

_____

_____

_____

_____

_____

_____

_____

_____

_____

_____

_____

_____

_____

CAMBRIDGE WRITING JOURNAL TEACHER'S RUBRIC

Rubric Standard	Grade 1-4 (4 is highest)	Specific Comments about this standard
Subject-Verb Agreement: Was there stellar *Subject-Verb* Agreement ?	/4	
Pronoun Usage: Was Pronoun Usage/Pronoun/Antecedent Agreement correct?	/4	
Vocabulary Integration: Was higher-level vocabulary used? Is the student making a good, concerted effort to use the vocabulary he/she has learned in his/her essay?	/4	
Unity & Coherence: Was the essay on topic and focused? Was there a logical progression of ideas from one to the next? Were there good transitions used in the essay to connect the different parts?	/4	
Sentence Structure and Variety: Did the essay display strong sentence structure *and* variety in sentence structure? Were there any fragments or run-on sentences?	/4	
Spelling and Correct Capitalization: How was the spelling and capitalization in the essay?	/4	
Good Opening and Closing: Were the opening and closing strong and well-stated?	/4	
Punctuation: How as the punctuation in the essay: commas, periods, semi-colors? Was it correctly implemented?	/4	
Depth of Thought and Critical Thinking: Did the student display good critical thinking, insight, and good depth of thought throughout the essay? Did he/she think "outside the box"?	/4	
Total Score	/36	

Other Feedback (Please comment on student's effort here)

_____

_____

_____

_____ .

WRITING PROMPT# _____ **Today's Date:**

_____

TOPIC/QUESTION/ PROMPT REFERENCE #:

_____

_____

_____

_____

_____

_____

_____

_____

_____

_____

_____

_____

_____

_____

_____

_____

_____

_____

CAMBRIDGE WRITING JOURNAL TEACHER'S RUBRIC

Rubric Standard	Grade 1-4 (4 is highest)	Specific Comments about this standard
Subject-Verb Agreement: Was there stellar *Subject-Verb* Agreement ?	/4	
Pronoun Usage: Was Pronoun Usage/Pronoun/Antecedent Agreement correct?	/4	
Vocabulary Integration: Was higher-level vocabulary used? Is the student making a good, concerted effort to use the vocabulary he/she has learned in his/her essay?	/4	
Unity & Coherence: Was the essay on topic and focused? Was there a logical progression of ideas from one to the next? Were there good transitions used in the essay to connect the different parts?	/4	
Sentence Structure and Variety: Did the essay display strong sentence structure *and* variety in sentence structure? Were there any fragments or run-on sentences?	/4	
Spelling and Correct Capitalization: How was the spelling and capitalization in the essay?	/4	
Good Opening and Closing: Were the opening and closing strong and well-stated?	/4	
Punctuation: How was the punctuation in the essay: commas, periods, semi-colors? Was it correctly implemented?	/4	
Depth of Thought and Critical Thinking: Did the student display good critical thinking, insight, and good depth of thought throughout the essay? Did he/she think "outside the box"?	/4	
Total Score	/36	

Other Feedback (Please comment on student's effort here)

_____

_____

WRITING PROMPT# _____ **Today's Date:** _____

TOPIC/QUESTION/ PROMPT REFERENCE #:

_____

_____

_____

_____

_____

_____

_____

_____

_____

_____

_____

_____

_____

_____

_____

CAMBRIDGE WRITING JOURNAL TEACHER'S RUBRIC

Rubric Standard	Grade 1-4 (4 is highest)	Specific Comments about this standard
Subject-Verb Agreement: Was there stellar *Subject-Verb* Agreement ?	/4	
Pronoun Usage: Was Pronoun Usage/Pronoun/Antecedent Agreement correct?	/4	
Vocabulary Integration: Was higher-level vocabulary used? Is the student making a good, concerted effort to use the vocabulary he/she has learned in his/her essay?	/4	
Unity & Coherence: Was the essay on topic and focused? Was there a logical progression of ideas from one to the next? Were there good transitions used in the essay to connect the different parts?	/4	
Sentence Structure and Variety: Did the essay display strong sentence structure *and* variety in sentence structure? Were there any fragments or run-on sentences?	/4	
Spelling and Correct Capitalization: How was the spelling and capitalization in the essay?	/4	
Good Opening and Closing: Were the opening and closing strong and well-stated?	/4	
Punctuation: How was the punctuation in the essay: commas, periods, semi-colors? Was it correctly implemented?	/4	
Depth of Thought and Critical Thinking: Did the student display good critical thinking, insight, and good depth of thought throughout the essay? Did he/she think "outside the box"?	/4	
Total Score	/36	

Other Feedback (Please comment on student's effort here)

_____

_____

_____

_____ .

WRITING PROMPT# _____ **Today's Date:**

_____

TOPIC/QUESTION/ PROMPT REFERENCE #:

_____

_____

_____

_____

_____

_____

_____

_____

_____

_____

_____

_____

_____

_____

_____

_____

_____

CAMBRIDGE WRITING JOURNAL TEACHER'S RUBRIC

Rubric Standard	Grade 1-4 (4 is highest)	Specific Comments about this standard
Subject-Verb Agreement: Was there stellar *Subject-Verb* Agreement ?	/4	
Pronoun Usage: Was Pronoun Usage/Pronoun/Antecedent Agreement correct?	/4	
Vocabulary Integration: Was higher-level vocabulary used? Is the student making a good, concerted effort to use the vocabulary he/she has learned in his/her essay?	/4	
Unity & Coherence: Was the essay on topic and focused? Was there a logical progression of ideas from one to the next? Were there good transitions used in the essay to connect the different parts?	/4	
Sentence Structure and Variety: Did the essay display strong sentence structure *and* variety in sentence structure? Were there any fragments or run-on sentences?	/4	
Spelling and Correct Capitalization: How was the spelling and capitalization in the essay?	/4	
Good Opening and Closing: Were the opening and closing strong and well-stated?	/4	
Punctuation: How was the punctuation in the essay: commas, periods, semi-colors? Was it correctly implemented?	/4	
Depth of Thought and Critical Thinking: Did the student display good critical thinking, insight, and good depth of thought throughout the essay? Did he/she think "outside the box"?	/4	
Total Score	/36	

Other Feedback (Please comment on student's effort here)

_____

_____

WRITING PROMPT#   **Today's Date:**

TOPIC/QUESTION/ PROMPT REFERENCE #:

CAMBRIDGE WRITING JOURNAL TEACHER'S RUBRIC

Rubric Standard	Grade 1-4 (4 is highest)	Specific Comments about this standard
Subject-Verb Agreement: Was there stellar *Subject-Verb* Agreement ?	/4	
Pronoun Usage: Was Pronoun Usage/Pronoun/Antecedent Agreement correct?	/4	
Vocabulary Integration: Was higher-level vocabulary used? Is the student making a good, concerted effort to use the vocabulary he/she has learned in his/her essay?	/4	
Unity & Coherence: Was the essay on topic and focused? Was there a logical progression of ideas from one to the next? Were there good transitions used in the essay to connect the different parts?	/4	
Sentence Structure and Variety: Did the essay display strong sentence structure *and* variety in sentence structure? Were there any fragments or run-on sentences?	/4	
Spelling and Correct Capitalization: How was the spelling and capitalization in the essay?	/4	
Good Opening and Closing: Were the opening and closing strong and well-stated?	/4	
Punctuation: How was the punctuation in the essay: commas, periods, semi-colors? Was it correctly implemented?	/4	
Depth of Thought and Critical Thinking: Did the student display good critical thinking, insight, and good depth of thought throughout the essay? Did he/she think "outside the box"?	/4	
Total Score	/36	

Other Feedback (Please comment on student's effort here)

_____

_____

WRITING PROMPT# _____ **Today's Date:**

_____

TOPIC/QUESTION/ PROMPT REFERENCE #:

_____

_____

_____

_____

_____

_____

_____

_____

_____

_____

_____

_____

_____

_____

_____

_____

CAMBRIDGE WRITING JOURNAL TEACHER'S RUBRIC

Rubric Standard	Grade 1-4 (4 is highest)	Specific Comments about this standard
Subject-Verb Agreement: Was there stellar *Subject-Verb* Agreement ?	/4	
Pronoun Usage: Was Pronoun Usage/Pronoun/Antecedent Agreement correct?	/4	
Vocabulary Integration: Was higher-level vocabulary used? Is the student making a good, concerted effort to use the vocabulary he/she has learned in his/her essay?	/4	
Unity & Coherence: Was the essay on topic and focused? Was there a logical progression of ideas from one to the next? Were there good transitions used in the essay to connect the different parts?	/4	
Sentence Structure and Variety: Did the essay display strong sentence structure *and* variety in sentence structure? Were there any fragments or run-on sentences?	/4	
Spelling and Correct Capitalization: How was the spelling and capitalization in the essay?	/4	
Good Opening and Closing: Were the opening and closing strong and well-stated?	/4	
Punctuation: How was the punctuation in the essay: commas, periods, semi-colors? Was it correctly implemented?	/4	
Depth of Thought and Critical Thinking: Did the student display good critical thinking, insight, and good depth of thought throughout the essay? Did he/she think "outside the box"?	/4	
Total Score	/36	

Other Feedback (Please comment on student's effort here)

_____

_____

_____ .
_____

WRITING PROMPT# _____   **Today's Date:**

_____

TOPIC/QUESTION/ PROMPT REFERENCE #:

_____

_____

_____

_____

_____

_____

_____

_____

_____

_____

_____

_____

_____

_____

_____

CAMBRIDGE WRITING JOURNAL TEACHER'S RUBRIC

Rubric Standard	Grade 1-4 (4 is highest)	Specific Comments about this standard
Subject-Verb Agreement: Was there stellar *Subject-Verb* Agreement ?	/4	
Pronoun Usage: Was Pronoun Usage/Pronoun/Antecedent Agreement correct?	/4	
Vocabulary Integration: Was higher-level vocabulary used? Is the student making a good, concerted effort to use the vocabulary he/she has learned in his/her essay?	/4	
Unity & Coherence: Was the essay on topic and focused? Was there a logical progression of ideas from one to the next? Were there good transitions used in the essay to connect the different parts?	/4	
Sentence Structure and Variety: Did the essay display strong sentence structure *and* variety in sentence structure? Were there any fragments or run-on sentences?	/4	
Spelling and Correct Capitalization: How was the spelling and capitalization in the essay?	/4	
Good Opening and Closing: Were the opening and closing strong and well-stated?	/4	
Punctuation: How was the punctuation in the essay: commas, periods, semi-colors? Was it correctly implemented?	/4	
Depth of Thought and Critical Thinking: Did the student display good critical thinking, insight, and good depth of thought throughout the essay? Did he/she think "outside the box"?	/4	
Total Score	/36	

Other Feedback (Please comment on student's effort here)

_____

_____

_____
_____ .

WRITING PROMPT# _____   **Today's Date:**

_____

TOPIC/QUESTION/ PROMPT REFERENCE #:

_____

_____

_____

_____

_____

_____

_____

_____

_____

_____

_____

_____

_____

_____

_____

_____

CAMBRIDGE WRITING JOURNAL TEACHER'S RUBRIC

Rubric Standard	Grade 1-4 (4 is highest)	Specific Comments about this standard
Subject-Verb Agreement: Was there stellar *Subject-Verb* Agreement ?	/4	
Pronoun Usage: Was Pronoun Usage/Pronoun/Antecedent Agreement correct?	/4	
Vocabulary Integration: Was higher-level vocabulary used? Is the student making a good, concerted effort to use the vocabulary he/she has learned in his/her essay?	/4	
Unity & Coherence: Was the essay on topic and focused? Was there a logical progression of ideas from one to the next? Were there good transitions used in the essay to connect the different parts?	/4	
Sentence Structure and Variety: Did the essay display strong sentence structure *and* variety in sentence structure? Were there any fragments or run-on sentences?	/4	
Spelling and Correct Capitalization: How was the spelling and capitalization in the essay?	/4	
Good Opening and Closing: Were the opening and closing strong and well-stated?	/4	
Punctuation: How was the punctuation in the essay: commas, periods, semi-colors? Was it correctly implemented?	/4	
Depth of Thought and Critical Thinking: Did the student display good critical thinking, insight, and good depth of thought throughout the essay? Did he/she think "outside the box"?	/4	
Total Score	/36	

Other Feedback (Please comment on student's effort here)

_____

_____

WRITING PROMPT#   **Today's Date:**

TOPIC/QUESTION/ PROMPT REFERENCE #:

CAMBRIDGE WRITING JOURNAL TEACHER'S RUBRIC

Rubric Standard	Grade 1-4 (4 is highest)	Specific Comments about this standard
Subject-Verb Agreement: Was there stellar *Subject-Verb* Agreement ?	/4	
Pronoun Usage: Was Pronoun Usage/Pronoun/Antecedent Agreement correct?	/4	
Vocabulary Integration: Was higher-level vocabulary used? Is the student making a good, concerted effort to use the vocabulary he/she has learned in his/her essay?	/4	
Unity & Coherence: Was the essay on topic and focused? Was there a logical progression of ideas from one to the next? Were there good transitions used in the essay to connect the different parts?	/4	
Sentence Structure and Variety: Did the essay display strong sentence structure *and* variety in sentence structure? Were there any fragments or run-on sentences?	/4	
Spelling and Correct Capitalization: How was the spelling and capitalization in the essay?	/4	
Good Opening and Closing: Were the opening and closing strong and well-stated?	/4	
Punctuation: How was the punctuation in the essay: commas, periods, semi-colors? Was it correctly implemented?	/4	
Depth of Thought and Critical Thinking: Did the student display good critical thinking, insight, and good depth of thought throughout the essay? Did he/she think "outside the box"?	/4	
Total Score	/36	

Other Feedback (Please comment on student's effort here)

_____

_____

WRITING PROMPT#   **Today's Date:**

TOPIC/QUESTION/ PROMPT REFERENCE #:

—

CAMBRIDGE WRITING JOURNAL TEACHER'S RUBRIC

Rubric Standard	Grade 1-4 (4 is highest)	Specific Comments about this standard
Subject-Verb Agreement: Was there stellar *Subject-Verb* Agreement ?	/4	
Pronoun Usage: Was Pronoun Usage/Pronoun/Antecedent Agreement correct?	/4	
Vocabulary Integration: Was higher-level vocabulary used? Is the student making a good, concerted effort to use the vocabulary he/she has learned in his/her essay?	/4	
Unity & Coherence: Was the essay on topic and focused? Was there a logical progression of ideas from one to the next? Were there good transitions used in the essay to connect the different parts?	/4	
Sentence Structure and Variety: Did the essay display strong sentence structure *and* variety in sentence structure? Were there any fragments or run-on sentences?	/4	
Spelling and Correct Capitalization: How was the spelling and capitalization in the essay?	/4	
Good Opening and Closing: Were the opening and closing strong and well-stated?	/4	
Punctuation: How was the punctuation in the essay: commas, periods, semi-colors? Was it correctly implemented?	/4	
Depth of Thought and Critical Thinking: Did the student display good critical thinking, insight, and good depth of thought throughout the essay? Did he/she think "outside the box"?	/4	
Total Score	/36	

Other Feedback (Please comment on student's effort here)

_____

_____

WRITING PROMPT#   **Today's Date:**

TOPIC/QUESTION/ PROMPT REFERENCE #:

CAMBRIDGE WRITING JOURNAL TEACHER'S RUBRIC

Rubric Standard	Grade 1-4 (4 is highest)	Specific Comments about this standard
Subject-Verb Agreement: Was there stellar *Subject-Verb* Agreement ?	/4	
Pronoun Usage: Was Pronoun Usage/Pronoun/Antecedent Agreement correct?	/4	
Vocabulary Integration: Was higher-level vocabulary used? Is the student making a good, concerted effort to use the vocabulary he/she has learned in his/her essay?	/4	
Unity & Coherence: Was the essay on topic and focused? Was there a logical progression of ideas from one to the next? Were there good transitions used in the essay to connect the different parts?	/4	
Sentence Structure and Variety: Did the essay display strong sentence structure *and* variety in sentence structure? Were there any fragments or run-on sentences?	/4	
Spelling and Correct Capitalization: How was the spelling and capitalization in the essay?	/4	
Good Opening and Closing: Were the opening and closing strong and well-stated?	/4	
Punctuation: How was the punctuation in the essay: commas, periods, semi-colors? Was it correctly implemented?	/4	
Depth of Thought and Critical Thinking: Did the student display good critical thinking, insight, and good depth of thought throughout the essay? Did he/she think "outside the box"?	/4	
Total Score	/36	

Other Feedback (Please comment on student's effort here)

_____

_____

_____
_____.

WRITING: GRAMMAR EXERCISE

TODAY'S DATE: _____

Teacher Directions:

_____

_____

****

_____
_____
_____
_____
_____
_____
_____
_____
_____
_____
_____
_____
_____
_____
_____
_____
_____
_____
_____

WRITING: GRAMMAR EXERCISE

TODAY'S DATE: _____

Teacher Directions:

_____

_____

****

_____
_____
_____

WRITING: GRAMMAR EXERCISE

TODAY'S DATE: _____

Teacher Directions:

_____

_____

****

_____
_____
_____
_____
_____
_____
_____
_____
_____
_____
_____
_____
_____
_____
_____
_____
_____
_____
_____
_____

_____

_____

_____

WRITING: GRAMMAR EXERCISE

TODAY'S DATE: _____

Teacher Directions:

_____

_____

****

_____

_____

_____

_____

_____

_____

_____

_____

_____

_____

_____

_____

_____

_____

_____

_____

_____

_____

_____

_____

_____

_____

_____
_____
_____

WRITING: GRAMMAR EXERCISE

TODAY'S DATE: _____

Teacher Directions:

_____

_____

****

_____
_____
_____
_____
_____
_____
_____
_____
_____
_____
_____
_____
_____
_____
_____
_____
_____
_____
_____

_____
_____

WRITING: GRAMMAR EXERCISE

TODAY'S DATE: _____

Teacher Directions:

_____

_____

****

_____
_____
_____
_____
_____
_____
_____
_____
_____
_____
_____
_____
_____
_____
_____
_____
_____
_____
_____
_____

_____
_____
_____

WRITING: GRAMMAR EXERCISE

TODAY'S DATE: _____

Teacher Directions:

_____

_____

****

_____
_____
_____
_____
_____
_____
_____
_____
_____
_____
_____
_____
_____
_____
_____
_____
_____
_____

_____

_____

_____

WRITING: GRAMMAR EXERCISE

TODAY'S DATE: _____

Teacher Directions:

_____

_____

****

_____

_____

_____

_____

_____

_____

_____

_____

_____

_____

_____

_____

_____

_____

_____

_____

_____

_____

_____
_____
_____

WRITING: GRAMMAR EXERCISE

TODAY'S DATE: _____

Teacher Directions:

_____

_____

****

_____
_____
_____
_____
_____
_____
_____
_____
_____
_____
_____
_____
_____
_____
_____
_____
_____
_____

_____
_____
_____

WRITING: GRAMMAR EXERCISE

TODAY'S DATE: _____

Teacher Directions:

_____

_____

****

_____
_____
_____
_____
_____
_____
_____
_____
_____
_____
_____
_____
_____
_____
_____
_____
_____
_____

_____
_____
_____

<u>WRITING: GRAMMAR EXERCISE</u>

TODAY'S DATE: _____

Teacher Directions:

_____
_____

****

_____
_____
_____
_____
_____
_____
_____
_____
_____
_____
_____
_____
_____
_____
_____
_____
_____
_____
_____
_____

_____
_____
_____

WRITING: GRAMMAR EXERCISE

TODAY'S DATE: _____

Teacher Directions:

_____

_____

****

_____
_____
_____
_____
_____
_____
_____
_____
_____
_____
_____
_____
_____
_____
_____
_____
_____

_____
_____

WRITING: GRAMMAR EXERCISE

TODAY'S DATE: _____

Teacher Directions:

_____
_____

****

_____
_____
_____
_____
_____
_____
_____
_____
_____
_____
_____
_____
_____
_____
_____
_____
_____
_____
_____
_____
_____
_____
_____

_____

_____

_____

WRITING: GRAMMAR EXERCISE

TODAY'S DATE: _____

Teacher Directions:

_____

_____

****

_____
_____
_____
_____
_____
_____
_____
_____
_____
_____
_____
_____
_____
_____
_____
_____
_____
_____
_____
_____

_____
_____
_____

WRITING: GRAMMAR EXERCISE

TODAY'S DATE: _____

Teacher Directions:

_____

_____

****

_____
_____
_____
_____
_____
_____
_____
_____
_____
_____
_____
_____
_____
_____
_____
_____
_____
_____
_____

_____
_____
_____

WRITING: GRAMMAR EXERCISE

TODAY'S DATE: _____

Teacher Directions:

_____
_____

****

_____
_____
_____
_____
_____
_____
_____
_____
_____
_____
_____
_____
_____
_____
_____
_____
_____

_____
_____

WRITING: GRAMMAR EXERCISE

TODAY'S DATE: _____

Teacher Directions:

_____
_____

****

_____
_____
_____
_____
_____
_____
_____
_____
_____
_____
_____
_____
_____
_____
_____
_____
_____
_____
_____
_____
_____

WRITING: GRAMMAR EXERCISE

TODAY'S DATE: _____

Teacher Directions:

_____

_____

****

_____
_____
_____
_____
_____
_____
_____
_____
_____
_____
_____
_____
_____
_____
_____
_____
_____

_____

_____

_____

WRITING: GRAMMAR EXERCISE

TODAY'S DATE: _____

Teacher Directions:

_____

_____

****

_____
_____
_____
_____
_____
_____
_____
_____
_____
_____
_____
_____
_____
_____
_____
_____
_____
_____
_____
_____
_____

WRITING: GRAMMAR EXERCISE

TODAY'S DATE: _____

Teacher Directions:

_____

_____

****

_____
_____
_____
_____
_____
_____
_____
_____
_____
_____
_____
_____
_____
_____
_____
_____
_____
_____

WRITING: GRAMMAR EXERCISE

TODAY'S DATE: _____

Teacher Directions:

_____

_____

****

_____
_____
_____
_____
_____
_____
_____
_____
_____
_____
_____
_____
_____
_____
_____
_____
_____

_____
_____
_____

<u>WRITING: GRAMMAR EXERCISE</u>

<u>TODAY'S DATE:</u> _____

Teacher Directions:

_____

_____

****

_____
_____
_____
_____
_____
_____
_____
_____
_____
_____
_____
_____
_____
_____
_____
_____
_____
_____
_____
_____

WRITING: GRAMMAR EXERCISE

TODAY'S DATE: _____

Teacher Directions:

_____

_____

****

_____
_____
_____
_____
_____
_____
_____
_____
_____
_____
_____
_____
_____
_____
_____
_____
_____
_____
_____
_____
_____
_____
_____

WRITING: GRAMMAR EXERCISE

TODAY'S DATE: _____

Teacher Directions:

_____

_____

****

_____
_____
_____
_____
_____
_____
_____
_____
_____
_____
_____
_____
_____
_____
_____
_____
_____
_____
_____
_____
_____
_____
_____

WRITING: GRAMMAR EXERCISE

TODAY'S DATE: _____

Teacher Directions:

_____

_____

****

_____
_____
_____
_____
_____
_____
_____
_____
_____
_____
_____
_____
_____
_____
_____
_____
_____
_____
_____
_____
_____
_____

WRITING: GRAMMAR EXERCISE

TODAY'S DATE: _____

Teacher Directions:

_____

_____

****

_____
_____
_____
_____
_____
_____
_____
_____
_____
_____
_____
_____
_____
_____
_____
_____
_____
_____
_____
_____
_____
_____
_____
_____
_____

WRITING: GRAMMAR EXERCISE

TODAY'S DATE: _____

Teacher Directions:

_____

_____

****

WRITING: GRAMMAR EXERCISE

TODAY'S DATE: _____

Teacher Directions:

_____

_____

****

_____
_____
_____
_____
_____
_____
_____
_____
_____
_____
_____
_____
_____
_____
_____
_____
_____
_____
_____
_____
_____
_____
_____

WRITING: GRAMMAR EXERCISE

TODAY'S DATE: _____

Teacher Directions:

_____

_____

****

_____
_____
_____
_____
_____
_____
_____
_____
_____
_____
_____
_____
_____
_____
_____
_____
_____
_____
_____
_____
_____
_____

WRITING: GRAMMAR EXERCISE

TODAY'S DATE: _____

Teacher Directions:

_____

_____

****

_____
_____
_____
_____
_____
_____
_____
_____
_____
_____
_____
_____
_____
_____
_____
_____
_____
_____
_____
_____
_____
_____

WRITING: GRAMMAR EXERCISE

TODAY'S DATE: _____

Teacher Directions:

_____

_____

****

_____
_____
_____
_____
_____
_____
_____
_____
_____
_____
_____
_____
_____
_____
_____
_____
_____
_____
_____
_____
_____
_____
_____

WRITING: GRAMMAR EXERCISE

TODAY'S DATE: _____

Teacher Directions:

_____

_____

****

_____
_____
_____
_____
_____
_____
_____
_____
_____
_____
_____
_____
_____
_____
_____
_____
_____
_____
_____
_____
_____
_____
_____
_____

WRITING: GRAMMAR EXERCISE

TODAY'S DATE: _____

Teacher Directions:

_____

_____

****

_____
_____
_____
_____
_____
_____
_____
_____
_____
_____
_____
_____
_____
_____
_____
_____
_____
_____
_____
_____
_____

WRITING: GRAMMAR EXERCISE

TODAY'S DATE: _____

Teacher Directions:

_____

_____

****

_____
_____
_____
_____
_____
_____
_____
_____
_____
_____
_____
_____
_____
_____
_____
_____
_____
_____
_____
_____
_____
_____
_____

WRITING: GRAMMAR EXERCISE

TODAY'S DATE: _____

Teacher Directions:

_____

_____

****

_____
_____
_____
_____
_____
_____
_____
_____
_____
_____
_____
_____
_____
_____
_____
_____
_____
_____
_____
_____
_____
_____

WRITING: GRAMMAR EXERCISE

TODAY'S DATE: _____

Teacher Directions:

_____

_____

****

_____
_____
_____
_____
_____
_____
_____
_____
_____
_____
_____
_____
_____
_____
_____
_____
_____
_____
_____
_____
_____
_____
_____

WRITING: GRAMMAR EXERCISE

TODAY'S DATE: _____

Teacher Directions:

_____

_____

****

_____
_____
_____
_____
_____
_____
_____
_____
_____
_____
_____
_____
_____
_____
_____
_____
_____
_____
_____
_____
_____
_____
_____

WRITING: GRAMMAR EXERCISE

TODAY'S DATE: _____

Teacher Directions:

_____

_____

****

_____
_____
_____
_____
_____
_____
_____
_____
_____
_____
_____
_____
_____
_____
_____
_____
_____
_____
_____
_____
_____

WRITING: GRAMMAR EXERCISE

TODAY'S DATE: _____

Teacher Directions:

_____

_____

****

_____
_____
_____
_____
_____
_____
_____
_____
_____
_____
_____
_____
_____
_____
_____
_____
_____
_____
_____
_____
_____
_____

WRITING: GRAMMAR EXERCISE

TODAY'S DATE: _____

Teacher Directions:

_____

_____

****

_____
_____
_____
_____
_____
_____
_____
_____
_____
_____
_____
_____
_____
_____
_____
_____
_____
_____
_____
_____
_____
_____
_____
_____

WRITING: GRAMMAR EXERCISE

TODAY'S DATE: _____

Teacher Directions:

_____

_____

****

_____
_____
_____
_____
_____
_____
_____
_____
_____
_____
_____
_____
_____
_____
_____
_____
_____
_____
_____
_____
_____
_____
_____

WRITING: GRAMMAR EXERCISE

TODAY'S DATE: _____

Teacher Directions:

_____

_____

****

_____
_____
_____
_____
_____
_____
_____
_____
_____
_____
_____
_____
_____
_____
_____
_____
_____
_____
_____
_____
_____
_____
_____
_____

WRITING: GRAMMAR EXERCISE

TODAY'S DATE: _____

Teacher Directions:

_____

_____

****

_____
_____
_____
_____
_____
_____
_____
_____
_____
_____
_____
_____
_____
_____
_____
_____
_____
_____
_____
_____
_____
_____
_____

WRITING: GRAMMAR EXERCISE

TODAY'S DATE: _____

Teacher Directions:

_____

_____

****

_____
_____
_____
_____
_____
_____
_____
_____
_____
_____
_____
_____
_____
_____
_____
_____
_____
_____
_____
_____
_____
_____
_____
_____

94975005R00143

Made in the USA
Columbia, SC
05 May 2018